JAMES SOUTHWELL

THIS BOOK BELONGS TO:

....

M ommy was reading the paper when she suddenly asked me, "Would you like a puppy?"

I was surprised. We had talked about it, but apparently it was more than just talk.

"Yes!" I exclaimed.

We got into the car and drove to the address where the puppies were.

I was very anxious to get there. How long is this car ride going to take? It seemed like forever, but we finally arrived.

A nice lady had a box sitting on the ground with four puppies in it. Three of the puppies were mostly white, and one was grey and white. The grey-and-white one looked smaller and weaker. But I did not care, he was perfect to me. I was thrilled when Daddy handed the puppy to me so I could hold him during the ride home.

I named my dog Harley. He often went to the bathroom where he was not supposed to and had to spend time kenneled in our kitchen. Once he became potty-trained, he was allowed in all of the carpeted areas of our home.

HARLEY

It was so much fun to play with my puppy inside the house. He quickly learned to do tricks. He could shake, roll over, sit, and walk on his hind legs. I would lie on the floor and roll with Harley playfully hopping on top of me. He would nibble on my ears or lick me.

Harley had his own basket of toys. He had various chew toys and balls. His favorite was a lamb with very long legs. It made a squeaky noise when he would bite it.

One day we entered Harley in a race for small dogs at a local dog track. Harley was a natural. He left all of the other dogs in the dust. He won several races to make it to the championship race. He easily won first place. It was thrilling to see him on the podium with his first place trophy.

About two months later, Harley had a serious accident. My dad hit him with a golf ball. We had to take him to a veterinarian to have surgery several times. Harley lost the use of his right front leg. My dad was very sad. I think he felt guilty.

Harley adjusted quickly and was soon running around with only three legs. He still played with me, and his toys, and even did most of his tricks. We even had him joining the dog race the following year. Do you know what Harley did? He won again!

Harley had the heart of a champion. He taught me that if something bad happens, you should not let it stop you. Keep trying and you can still achieve your goals.

About the Author

James Southwell is a teacher in the PSJA ISD. He lives with his wife, son and new dog, Piper.